THE AZTECS

BY
BY
JOHN D. CLARE

WHO WERE THE AZTECS?

A WELCOME SIGN

The Mexica were nomads but in about 1300, they settled in a town named Culhuacan. There they sacrificed a local nobleman's daughter, and cut off all her skin. The local people were horrified and drove them out, so they fled to a nearby swamp. The next day, they saw the sign they had been waiting for – an eagle, on a cactus, eating a snake. They settled in the swamp, and built the town of Tenochtitlan (Place of the Prickly Pear) in about 1100.

In 1519, the mighty Aztec Empire covered 200,000 sq km of land, and contained at least three million people who spoke more than 20 different languages. Tenochtitlan, the capital, was one of the biggest and most beautiful cities in the world. The Aztecs never called themselves Aztecs (although we will call them that in this book). They were the Mexica – nomads who invaded the area we now call Mexico in about 1100. But they did not settle in Tenochtitlan until 1325. Aztec culture grew, flowered and died in less than two centuries.

CHANGING IDENTITY

Izcoatl, the first imperial Aztec ruler, disliked the idea that his people were barbaric nomads, and destroyed all the writings that said so. Instead, the Aztecs claimed that they originally came from Aztlan, which is where the Toltecs came from. Huitzilopochtli, the god of war (shown right), told them to find a new home. They would know the place, said the god, when they saw an eagle, on a cactus, eating a snake.

FIERCE BEAUTY

Historians are puzzled by the Aztecs' culture. In some ways it was colourful and beautiful, but it was also bloody and barbaric. This turquoise mask is beautifully made, but was used in an evil purpose. It would probably have been worn by priests in rituals.

TOLTEC TEMPLES

When the Aztecs settled in Mexico, they found the remains of past civilizations. They discovered Toltec temple ruins, which contained huge statues, like the one shown here at Tula, the Toltec capital. This architecture amazed the Aztecs, who decided to copy the ways of these ancient peoples. In 1427, they asked Izcoatl, a local prince who claimed to be descended from the Toltecs, to be their ruler.

AZTEC EXPANSION

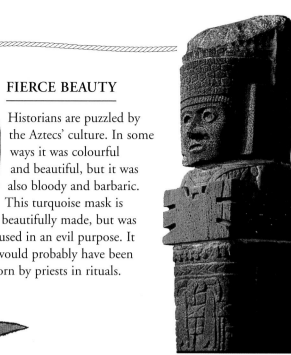

There was no farmland, wood or stone in Tenochtitlan, but there was salt (important in a hot country) and water. There were birds, fish and frogs to eat. Slowly the Aztecs grew more powerful, and conquered neighbouring peoples. The Aztecs liked to pretend that they had a great empire, but they were never all-powerful. They ruled with the help of two other cities, Texcoco and Tlacopan, and there were some towns that they never conquered. This picture shows warriors from Tlaxcala successfully fighting off an Aztec attack.

THE AZTEC EMPIRE

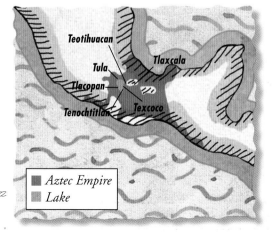

This map shows the Aztec Empire at its greatest. The Aztecs ruled directly over the Valley of Mexico around Tenochtitlan, but they also controlled surrounding tribes. They let tribal leaders rule over their own people, but they demanded large tributes (payments) from them in exchange.

Teotihuacan
Tula
Tlaxcala
Tlacopan
Tenochtitlan
Texcoco

■ Aztec Empire
■ Lake

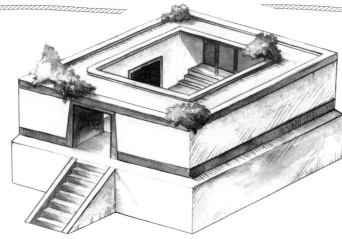

A NOBLEMAN'S HOUSE

There were only a few nobles in Aztec society. They had special privileges that were fiercely protected by law. Only nobles could live in two-storey houses, for example. Any commoner who pretended to be a noble was sentenced to death.

GOLDEN MYTHOLOGY

A nobleman was expected to be a good citizen, and there were strict laws that could be used against noblemen who behaved badly. This means some of them must have misbehaved. This gold pendant gives a clue as to why they did this. It shows Mictlantecuhtli, the lord of the dead, who ruled the hells under the Earth. Souls who reached the land of Mictlantecuhtli were destroyed forever, so some nobles decided to have fun while they were alive. An Aztec poem says: "We are only here on Earth for a while, come let us enjoy ourselves."

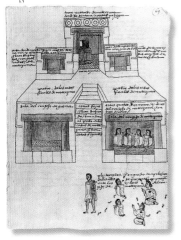

MOCTEZUMA'S PALACE

This Aztec drawing shows Moctezuma's palace in Tenochtitlan. Inside, Moctezuma sits alone in the throne room, while below are the meeting rooms for his generals (left) and his advisers (right). Moctezuma's officials (tecuhtli) were expected to work, but in return they were given a fine house and lands, paid large salaries and did not pay taxes. The most important was a man called the Snake Woman (named after an important goddess). He was the chief minister who looked after the everyday affairs of government. In the Aztec Empire, only the nobles (the pipiltin) could become government officials.

LIFE FOR THE RICH

The Aztecs conquered many cities, which were then forced to pay tribute. This meant that huge amounts of valuable goods came to Tenochtitlan. These included, military outfits, beads, feathers, dyes, gold, cotton, peppers and spices, sacks of maize and cacao beans, salt and many other things. Some of these were used in public ceremonies, some were given to the nobles and some were given to the local merchants, who traded them for other goods. Tenochtitlan soon grew into a very wealthy city.

MOCTEZUMA II

At the head of Aztec society was the tlatoani. He was king, chief priest and commander of the army. In 1502, Moctezuma II became the ninth tlatoani of Tenochtitlan. Nobles who went to see him had to take off their fine clothes and put on cheap blankets. They had to enter barefoot, with eyes lowered, and bow three times, saying: "My Lord, my great Lord!" Turning their backs on him was forbidden; instead, they had to walk out backwards. Moctezuma II ruled from 1503, until he was murdered in 1520.

A NOBLEMAN

Noblemen either inherited their titles or could be given them if they became a Jaguar or Eagle warrior knight. Moctezuma stopped this practice, however.

TRIBUTE ROLL

Tribute rolls showed the amount and type of taxes that had to be paid by provinces to the Aztec capital. The Aztecs used symbols for numbers – a dot meant 1, a flag meant 20 and a feather was 400. The various symbols showed the type of goods that were to be sent to Tenochtitlan.

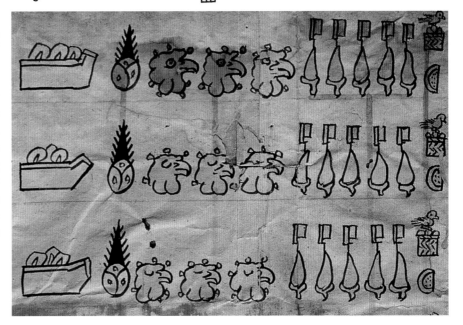

LIFE FOR THE POOR

HOUSEHOLD GODS

In every home, mothers made a shrine of dough to imitate the temple pyramids (see pages 30-31). They burned incense and offered food to copy the rituals at the temple. These figurines may have represented gods, but they are often found with their heads deliberately broken off, so they may have represented victims who were 'sacrificed' at the household shrine.

*A*ztec society had a strict class system. The tlatoani was at the top, with the pipiltin (nobles) below him, followed by the macehualtin (citizens). The macehualtin were free, although the word means 'subjects'. They were organized into calpulli (groups) of about 100 households. Each calpulli had a council of elders who kept the register of citizens, shared out the land and collected taxes. Nothing ever changed; people stayed in the class into which they were born and Aztec children were cut on the chest to show which calpulli they came from.

PEASANT HOUSING

Aztec peasant houses were built in groups of up to five, and faced each other round a courtyard. They had mud-brick walls and roofs thatched with leaves from plants. More than one family might live in the house. The houses were very small and most activities, including cooking and eating, spinning, grinding corn and socializing, would have taken place outside.

SLAVES

At the bottom of society came the slaves (the tlacotin). Slaves were given as tributes by conquered cities. Some were criminals whose punishment was to be made slaves. Sometimes peasants, ruined by drink, gambling or disaster, would sell themselves into slavery in exchange for a loan to the rest of the family. Slaves could only be sold on if they were lazy – but the third time this happened, they were sold to the temple for sacrifice! This picture shows Chalchiuhtlicue, goddess of water, being attended to by slaves.

PEASANT POSSESSIONS

Poor families had little furniture and only simple clothes. They owned a metate stone for grinding maize, some pots and a sleeping mat. However, archaeologists have now dug up large piles of rubbish outside peasants' houses, including imported pottery, obsidian (a glassy type of volcanic rock) knives, grinding stones and even bronze pins. Aztec peasants could find plenty of work, and goods continued to flow into the empire.

ESSENTIAL POTS

Even the poorest Aztec families needed pots – a water jar, a bowl for soaking maize, a flat grid for cooking, storage jars, plates and cups. Also needed was at least one three-legged cajete with a crisscross pattern on the bottom, for grating chillies.

A HARD LIFE

The macehualtin produced the food, built the roads, temples and palaces and did extra work for the nobles. They paid taxes to the government officials to maintain the temples and schools, and they gave to charity to help the widows and orphans. Half of Moctezuma's income came from the ordinary macehualtin who were not allowed by law to wear fine clothes.

FOOD AND DRINK

FAVOURITE FOODS

The Aztecs ate a surprisingly varied range of food. Particular favourites included kidney beans, sweet potatoes, avocados, maize, squash, chilli peppers, red, yellow and green peppers, tomatoes, mushrooms, duck, fish, rabbit and snails.

The Aztecs were expert farmers. Most houses had a large garden (calmil). The tlatoani even had a botanical garden, where his gardeners grew plants such as tropical flowers and cacao trees. There were no horses, oxen, wheeled carts or ploughs, so everything had to be done by hand. In the hills, the Aztecs built stone walls and made flat terraces for growing crops. In the hot valleys, they built aqueducts to bring water from the mountains. The tlatoani controlled all the water, which was one reason he was so powerful. The Aztecs' diet included things that seem surprisingly modern, such as popcorn, hot chocolate and roasted peanuts.

PULQUE GOBLET

By law, only old women were allowed to get drunk, but at weddings people got merry on pulque, an alcoholic drink made from maguey sap (see opposite). The rich enjoyed a drink made by boiling cacao (known to us as cocoa) beans and honey. Some rich Aztecs also smoked tobacco, holding their nose and sucking in the smoke.

GROWING MAIZE

Maize was the main food in the Aztecs' diet and was planted each May. The farmer made holes with a stick called a coa and dropped in each seed individually. In July, all but the best ears were picked from each plant. The full-grown cobs were harvested in September. The maize was ground into flour and made into round, flat cakes called tortillas, which were eaten with every meal.

CHINAMPAS

In the swamps around Tenochtitlan, the Aztecs dredged mud from the bottom of the lake and piled it up to make allotments called chinampas. Along the edges, they grew willow trees to make strong banks. The lake also provided a good source of fish, waterfowl and even blue-green algae, which was made into small cakes.

MAGUEY PLANTS

The maguey plant was important for the Aztecs. The tough stems made good firewood or strong fence posts. Its leaves were used as fuel for fires and also for thatching roofs. The leaf fibres were used to make the rough cloth worn by the peasants, and also for rope, paper, sandals, nets, bags and blankets. Maguey sap was used to make a sweet syrup, or for pulque, and the spines made perfect nails and needles. Even the grubs that ate the leaves were a tasty treat!

FOOD FROM THE GODS

The Aztecs believed that all food was given by the gods, and held three festivals to help the maize grow. In May, the seed was blessed in the temple of Chicomecoatl, the goddess of corn, seen here with one of her attendants. In July, the young cobs were offered to Xilonen, a maize goddess. In September, a harvest festival was held, when a priestess dressed as Chicomecoatl threw dried seed at the crowds. People tried to catch some to add to the seeds they were keeping for the following year.

PASTIMES

VOLADOR CEREMONY

In this sacred performance four men dressed up as birds, since it was believed the gods themselves could take this form. The men swung round the pole on ropes which gradually unwound and lowered them to the ground. The length of the ropes was calculated so that they reached the ground in a total of 52 revolutions. The sacred number 52 symbolized the years in a full 'Calendar Round', equivalent to one of our centuries.

*R*eligion was central in the lives of the Aztecs. Everything they did had a religious meaning. Aztecs did not do activities just to enjoy themselves. Although Aztec adults enjoyed the festivals and games mentioned here, simply having fun was not their aim. The way they behaved and the things they did all had to fit in the will of the gods.

AZTEC ORCHESTRA

Most Aztec music involved community chanting and stamping to the beat. The main instrument was the huehuetl vertical drum, and its name (pronounced way-waytl) gives a clue to the sound it made. Another important instrument was the teponaztli, a horizontal round drum, which was hit with rubber-tipped sticks to make two different-sounding tones.

PLAYTIME

Aztec children were only allowed to play with their toys until they were three or four years old. After that, boys had to fetch the water, and girls had to help their mothers around the house.

POETRY OF LIFE

Nahuatl was the Aztecs' language. The Nahuatl word for poetry meant 'flower-and-song'. Much Aztec poetry was written to the god Tezcatlipoca, the giver and taker of life. In many poems, the ideas of flowers and song and life and death are linked: 'You come out from the flower and song; You scatter the flowers, You destroy them.' This painting shows Xochipilli, god of music, poetry, dancing and flowers. The Nahuatl word xochitl does actually mean 'flower'.

BALL GAMES

Tlachtli was a game in which players used their hips, knees and elbows to strike a large, rubber ball. If a player hit the ball through one of the raised hoops on the side of the court, he won. Tlachtli was a popular spectator sport, but it had religious meaning and losers were sometimes sacrificed. The game was also used to tell the future. When the ruler of Texcoco prophesized that strangers would soon rule Mexico, Moctezuma played tlachtli with him to prove he was wrong. Moctezuma lost the game 3-2, and left the court a worried man. Two years later, in 1519, the Spanish arrived.

PATOLLI

Patolli was a gambling board-game. Players threw dice to move, and the aim was to get three counters in a row. Even this simple game had a sacred meaning, since the board was made up of 52 sections, another reminder of the significance of the calendar. This picture shows a game being watched by Macuilxochitl, the god of plants and fun.

HAIRSTYLES

Aztec women loved to dress their hair, and dyed it black with mud or deep violet blue using indigo. The usual hairstyle was two plaits, brought round the front of the head and fastened together at the forehead. However, this statue of an Aztec goddess shows another style. The hair is gathered into bunches at the side of the head and worn with a braided headband. Hairstyles were important for Aztec men, too. Young men aged between 10 and 15 shaved their head, leaving only a pigtail at the back. They were only allowed to cut off the pigtail when they captured a prisoner in battle.

MAKE-UP MIRROR

This mirror is made of obsidian, a black volcanic glass. Aztec fathers told their daughters not to be vain, and not to use make-up – but they were ignored! The Aztecs used make-up in a very dramatic way. The face and body were thickly painted red, yellow, blue or green. For Aztec women, the fashionable colour was yellow, and they rubbed their faces with a yellow ointment called axin, made from the crushed bodies of insects. They also stained their teeth bright red.

NOBLE DRESS

This nobleman wears a coloured cotton cloak, decorated loincloth, sandals and an expensive necklace. Rich men sometimes wore many cloaks, one on top of the other, to show off their wealth.

FINE FEATHERS

Feathers were such an important part of a noble's costume that they formed part of most tribute rolls (see page 5), and feather-working was a major industry. This picture shows Moctezuma's headdress. The feathers were pushed into bamboo tubes, and sewn together using a thread made of cactus fibres.

FASHION

The Aztecs did not have fashion just to look attractive or up-to-date. In the Aztec Empire, dress, like everything else, had a meaning – it told the world about someone's wealth and status. What an Aztec could wear was set down by law. The macehualtin were forbidden to wear coloured cloaks, cotton cloth or gold jewellery. If a person ever wore a robe longer than the law allowed, his legs would be inspected – if these showed battle scars, the matter was dropped, but if they did not, he was put to death. Most poor people wore only a loincloth. If they could afford a cloak, it had to be a rough, white blanket made from the maguey plant.

USEFUL COTTON

Cotton could not be grown in Tenochtitlan, so it had to be imported from low-lying areas of Central America. As well as being an important fabric for clothes-making, cotton was used for bedding, bags, wall hangings, battle dress and burial shrouds.

JEWELLERY

Aztec nobles wore as much jewellery as possible – lip plugs, nose rings and earrings of gold and precious stones. This earring has a gold skull with tiny bells hanging from it.

TEOTIHUACAN STONEWORK

Five hundred years before the arrival of the Aztecs, a great city had existed in the Valley of Mexico. It was called Teotihuacan, and was about 80 km north-east of Tenochtitlan. When the Aztecs migrated to Mexico, they saw the city's ruins and were so impressed that they decided it was the birthplace of the gods. They adopted many things from Teotihuacan, including its pyramids, its gods Tlaloc and Quetzalcoatl, and the practice of human sacrifice. Rich Aztec nobles would decorate their palaces with stone carvings just like the designs found in Teotihuacan, seen in this picture.

THE TEMPLE AREA

This drawing shows the temple area in Tenochtitlan.

This was the main temple, with its twin shrines to Tlaloc, the god of water (on the left) and Huitzilopochtli, the god of war (on the right).

A GRUESOME GODDESS

This statue represents the awesome goddess Coatlicue, the mother of Huitzilopochtli (god of war), so its symbolism is gruesome. She wears a necklace made of a skull, hands and human hearts, her skirt is a mass of snakes and her feet are huge animal claws. Where her head has been cut off – blood pours out in the form of serpents.

The temple of Quetzalcoatl (the god of priests) is in the centre, with rings like the coils of a snake.

The priests' quarters. This building also housed the calmecac school (see page 20).

ART AND ARCHITECTURE

STONEWORKERS

Aztec quarrymen could cut 40-tonne slabs of rock by driving wooden wedges down cracks in the rock. Teams of labourers then dragged them to the building site, where they polished them and used metal chisels to carve the details.

*A*ztec art and architecture was designed to remind people of the power of the gods and the strength of the Aztec Empire. The Aztec capital Tenochtitlan became a city calculated to impress strangers. Reached by three causeways, which crossed the lake from the mainland, Tenochtitlan was built on a grid pattern, with the main street running east to west, copying the movement of the sun across the sky. Aztecs believed it was the centre of the Earth.

The small platform was for gladiatorial sacrifices. A captured warrior would be tied there and given a wooden club. A fully-armed Aztec warrior would then fight him to the death.

The skull rack was next to the tlachtli court. One Spaniard worked out that the rack contained 136,000 skulls of sacrificial victims.

The tlachtli court was situated next to the temple of Quetzalcoatl.

GRASSHOPPER

This pretty grasshopper was a symbol of Chapultepec ('Grasshopper Hill'), just north of Tenochtitlan. The Aztecs stopped here during their time of wandering (see page 3). Chapultepec was also important to the Aztecs because of its springs of fresh water, which were taken by aqueduct to Tenochtitlan.

HEALTH AND MEDICINE

Tenochtitlan had no working animals and its houses were built a good distance apart, so it was a healthier place to live in than European cities of this period. The Aztecs also had a good standard of personal hygiene. They washed often, using the soap-tree fruit to clean themselves. Moctezuma had a swimming bath in his palace, while many ordinary families had small bath-houses. Aztecs cleaned their teeth using salt and powdered charcoal, for they knew that otherwise their teeth would decay. They also checked each other's hair for lice. If someone became ill, the Aztecs had trained doctors who examined the symptoms and then prescribed a cure.

AZTEC DOCTORS

Aztec doctors could carry out a range of treatments, such as massaging aches, stopping bleeding, stitching up wounds and setting broken bones. However, they believed that it was an evil spirit that had caused the patient to stumble, so as they set the bone they chanted a spell.

GODS OF DISEASE

The Aztecs believed that most diseases were punishments from the gods. This picture shows Tlaloc, the god of water, who was thought to send diseases, such as leprosy and ulcers, on the cold winds.

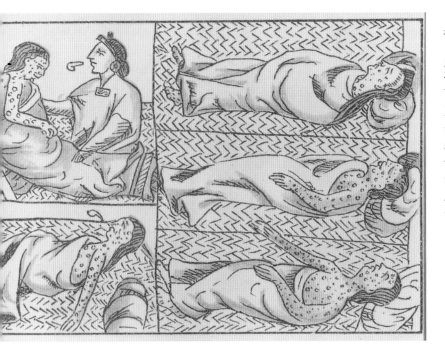

SMALLPOX

When the Spaniards came to Mexico, they brought with them new diseases, such as smallpox, to which the Aztecs were not immune. This caused the deaths of millions of native Aztecs in the years after the Spanish conquest.

MEDICINAL PLANTS

A good Aztec doctor knew how to use more than 1,500 herbal medicines. To treat a sore throat, for example, the doctor would prescribe a throat massage with liquid rubber, followed by a cough syrup made of honey and the syrup of the maguey plant.

FATES IN THE CRADLE

This picture shows the beautiful goddess Chalchiuhtlicue, the wife of Tlaloc and the goddess of clean water and childbirth. The Aztecs believed the fate of a child depended on the day it was born, and that some children were destined to be sickly and others to be healthy.

MAGICAL CURES

To diagnose a disease, doctors often gave a dose of peyotl. This would cause the patient to become delirious and cry out, thus 'revealing' the cause of the disease. If the cause was thought to be the anger of the gods, the cure would usually be prayers and a symbolic medicine, such as crushed quartz or the spray of a skunk. If the cause was an enemy's magic, known as 'worm-drawers', doctors would rub the affected spot, 'pull out' a stone or a worm from the patient and declare the patient healed.

LOVE AND MARRIAGE

Girls in Aztec society would normally marry in their late teens. On the day of the wedding, the girl's parents gave a feast. The bride bathed, washed her hair and put on her wedding clothes. When it was dark, the marriage procession set off for the groom's house. Women with burning torches led the way, and the matchmaker carried the bride on her back. Once there, the matchmaker 'tied the knot' – actually tying the man's cloak to the girl's blouse.

*M*arriage was important in Aztec society, and an unmarried man could not become a citizen. Men were allowed to have as many wives as they could afford to support. Marriages were arranged by the parents, who decided on future matches when their children were still young. An older woman acted as a matchmaker, asking permission for the marriage from the girl's parents. After marriage, roles for men and women were very clear. The man built the house and earned the wages. A woman's job was to run the home.

XOCHIQUETZAL

Xochiquetzal was the goddess of love, the Earth, flowers and plants, games and dance. She was also the patroness of artisans (skilled workers), pregnant women and childbirth. Her name means 'flower feather'. Xochiquetzal was a young, beautiful and charming goddess. She was often shown with butterflies and birds flying around her, with a hummingbird or an ocelot, a leopard-like animal. Every eight years, the Aztecs held a feast in honour of Xochiquetzal, with guests wearing animal and flower masks.

MARRIED COUPLES

Women had separate roles to men, but they were not treated badly. Men spent much of the year working away from home, and during this time their wives were in charge of the household. A woman could divorce a husband who abandoned her or was violent, and the law gave her half his land and possessions. Although marriages were arranged, most couples grew to love each other and were happy. This picture shows a man and wife sharing the important job of storing the maize.

AZTEC WOMEN

Aztec women cleaned the house, made the meals, wove cloth and looked after the children. Sweeping was seen as a vital religious duty – Aztec women believed it helped the gods to purify the world. "Take care of the sweeping. Get up in the deep of night to look after the house," elders told a woman on her wedding day.

NEW ARRIVALS

Aztec couples wanted children, and a childless marriage usually ended in divorce. During the birth, the midwife shouted out battle cries, as the mother 'fought' to bring the child into the world. Astrologers were consulted to foretell the child's future based on its birthday. As the midwife cut the umbilical cord, she spoke to the new baby. If it was a boy, she told him that he must be a great warrior, who would feed the sun with his enemies' blood. A girl was instructed to devote her life to looking after the home.

CHILDREN

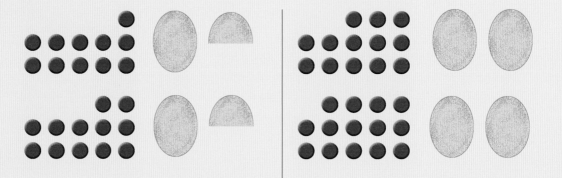

The law required every calpulli, or group of households, to build schools for teenagers. Girls were taught how to sing and dance at the religious festivals, while boys helped with building work and trained to be soldiers. Noblemen's sons went to advanced schools known as calmecacs, where they learned about war and religion, but also studied history, medicine, mathematics, the calendar, astrology and law. There were strict rules for behaviour. Boys were not allowed to drink. Aztec girls were expected to be modest, and had to look down at the floor at all times. Aztec education taught children to obey. They were made to think like everyone else, not for themselves. No one was allowed to be different.

PUNISHMENTS

Punishments for Aztec children were very harsh. This father is holding his son over a fire and forcing him to breathe in the fumes of burning chilli peppers. The speech comma tells us that the child is also being given a long lecture as he is being punished.

SYMBOLS

The *Codex Mendoza* was a collection of drawings of native customs and tributes put together for the viceroy of Spain after the Conquest. The pictures in the *Codex* about bringing up children (shown on page 21) use the following key to show age and food. The red counters show the age of the child and the yellow chips show the number of tortillas they were allowed to eat in a day.

A BOY'S EDUCATION

Education for Aztec boys centred on learning skills that they would need in later life. They also needed to be able to operate boats and canoes in order to work on the chinampas.

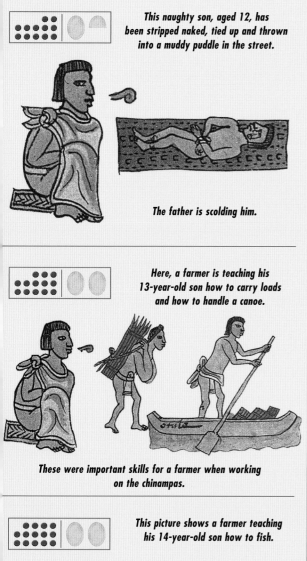

This naughty son, aged 12, has been stripped naked, tied up and thrown into a muddy puddle in the street.

The father is scolding him.

Here, a farmer is teaching his 13-year-old son how to carry loads and how to handle a canoe.

These were important skills for a farmer when working on the chinampas.

This picture shows a farmer teaching his 14-year-old son how to fish.

At this age, the boy would have been eating two tortillas a day, so it was important that he earned a living.

A GIRL'S EDUCATION

Most Aztec education for girls took place in the home. From an early age, a girl would be taught skills that she would use daily in her role as a homemaker in later life.

At age 12, a daughter would be taught to grind maize and make tortillas – the first job she would do every morning when she became a mother herself.

At age 13, this girl is being taught how to sweep the floor. Sweeping was seen as a religious duty.

Aztec women believed that when they swept up, they were helping the gods to purify the world.

Weaving was a woman's job in the Aztec Empire. Here, the mother is teaching the 14-year-old girl how to use a backstrap loom.

She has attached one end to the wall, and has strapped the other end round her back. By moving backwards and forwards, she can tighten or loosen the threads.

WAR AND WEAPONS

A DEADLY CEREMONY

The Aztecs went to war not simply to conquer other peoples and gain tribute, but also to capture victims for sacrifice. In the ceremony shown in this Aztec painting, the captives were forced to dance all night, and were burned at the stake the next morning.

The Aztecs were a fierce, military people who glorified war. The growth of the Aztec Empire depended on war. Its history said that the god of war, Huitzilopochtli, had told the Aztecs to leave Aztlan and conquer the land. The empire's success and wealth depended on tribute payments from conquered cities. The Aztecs believed that the gods needed a constant supply of blood sacrifices to keep the world from falling apart, and wars were a good way to provide the victims.

PROTECTION

A warrior's shield was probably made of wood covered with leather, and decorated with feathers stuck on with bat-dung glue. It would probably have given only limited protection during battle.

DRESSED TO KILL

Each calpulli sent a regiment of men to fight in the army. There was no uniform; each soldier dressed as he wanted. This warrior wears sandals, a coloured skirt, a feather headdress and a thick, quilted, cotton bodysuit. He would probably have removed everything except the bodysuit and sandals before fighting. He carries a thick, two-sided weapon, called a maquahuitl, that was so effective it could cut off a man's head with one blow.

THE MILITARY ELITE

The two highest Aztec military orders were the Jaguar knights and the Eagle knights. Only warriors who had taken many captives could belong. They were given extra land and privileges, and took a special part in the ceremonial dances when captives were sacrificed. This ceramic figure is a life-sized sculpture of an Eagle knight. It was found by archaeologists in the Eagle House next to the Great Temple in Tenochtitlan.

DANGEROUS MISSILES

Aztec commanders often started a battle with a hail of spears. This picture shows two Aztec spear-throwers, or atlatls. Soldiers used these like a sling; once the spear was placed in the atlatl's groove, it could be thrown with great force.

WAR OF FLOWERS

One of the strangest Aztec activities was xochiyaotl, or the 'War of Flowers'. The warriors fought to show their skill and to take captives from their rivals' community, rather than killing each other. Afterwards, the captives would be sacrificed, and their arms and legs would be given to the victorious Aztec soldiers to take home and eat. This was seen as a way of sharing their life-blood with Huitzilopochtli.

TRADE AND TRAVEL

Aztecs loved going to the market (tianquiz) – 60,000 people went to the great market of Tlatelolco (just outside Tenochtitlan) every day. One Spanish priest wrote that, 'given the choice between going to market and going to heaven, the normal Aztec housewife chose heaven, but asked if she could go to the market first!' The Aztecs were extensive traders, and their merchants (pochteca) were a separate class within Aztec society, each owning their own calpulli. They also had their own god, Yacatecuhtli, whose symbol was a traveller's walking stick. But the Aztec pochteca could not become noblemen. They had to keep to their place within Aztec society.

MONEY BEANS

The Aztecs didn't have actual money and used cacao beans as a way to trade. Some criminals made forgeries out of wax or dough.

AZTEC SHOPPING

This picture shows an Aztec tianquiz in Tlaxcala. Goods, such as meat, vegetables and herbs were arranged in separate aisles, a little like a modern supermarket. Customers could buy not only the produce of the chinampas (see page 9), but also other foodstuffs, which included dogs, iguana and wild turkeys from the valleys and oysters, crabs and turtles from the coast. They could also buy many other things, from cotton and slaves to shells and gold. The Aztecs sold by quantity rather than by weight. Traders and customers usually bartered for goods, so the tianquiz must have been very noisy. Government inspectors made sure goods were set out properly, and cheats were punished.

NOBLE TRANSPORT

The Aztecs had no horses, so a common form of transport, for nobles and rich traders, was the litter. Here, an important person dressed as an Eagle Warrior is being carried on a litter in a religious procession.

PORTERS

Trading expeditions could be very dangerous. The pochteca were the only people allowed to cross borders into other states, as the government found them useful as spies. Traders took weapons, and sometimes ended up fighting the people with whom they had gone to trade. Everything had to be carried, and the Aztecs used porters who – like the one here – wore head-straps rather than backpacks to bear the load. Before they set off, the pochteca would meet together and make offerings to the gods, asking for continued health and safety.

CANOES

Though they knew the principle of the wheel, the Aztecs did not use wheeled vehicles. Canoes were therefore essential for carrying heavy goods into Tenochtitlan, and the canals were the city's main 'streets'. Destroying Aztec traders' canoes was regarded as a declaration of war. After an expedition, the pochteca would smuggle their goods secretly into the city at night. Aztec commoners were not supposed to flaunt how rich they were. Merchants wore simple clothes and kept secret how much wealth they possessed.

LIZARD

SERPENT

EAGLE

RABBIT

WATER

DOG

MONKEY

GRASS

REED

OCELOT

SCIENCE AND TECHNOLOGY

The Aztecs had no alphabet, but used picture symbols called glyphs instead. These were also used to represent the 20 days of the Sacred Calendar (shown on the left and right-hand borders). But the Aztecs were also very skilled at making beautiful things. One of the first Spaniards to reach Tenochtitlan wrote: "It is like the enchantments they tell of in the old legends!" One historian said the Aztecs were successful because they learned to use simple tools with great skill.

AZTEC POTTERY

Aztec potters did not use a wheel; instead, they built up layers of rolled clay, and then crafted the pot with their fingers. They had no knowledge of glazes; most Aztec pottery made in Moctezuma's time had black designs painted directly onto the clay surface. Rich Aztecs, however, preferred to use pottery made by the non-Aztec people of Cholula, a city 160 km east of Tenochtitlan. Cholulan pottery was multicoloured, and included drawings of feathers, knives and skulls.

ANIMAL MAGIC

Aztec stoneworkers made jewellery and religious figurines out of alabaster, jade, turquoise, amber and obsidian. The stoneworkers of Tenochtitlan persuaded Moctezuma to go to war against certain cities, to provide the emery sand they used for polishing the stones. The Aztecs loved nature, and animals were a favourite subject for carvings, like this beautiful pot in the form of a hare.

CALENDAR STONE

The Aztecs did not have a scientific explanation of how the world was created. They believed that there had been four failed 'worlds' before the present age, and that the gods Tezcatlipoca, Quetzalcoatl, Tlaloc and Chalchiuhtlicue had each in turn become the sun, but had then been destroyed. The Aztecs believed that they were living in the 'fifth sun'. This huge, 24 tonne 'Calendar Stone' (left) measuring almost 4 metres across, shows the fifth sun, Tonatiuh, at the centre. The four squares around this stand for the four 'failed' suns.

THE LOST-WAX METHOD

Gold jewellery was made using a special technique called the 'lost-wax' method. First, a model was made from charcoal and covered in beeswax. The model was then coated in a paste of charcoal and clay. As the hot metal was poured into the mould, the wax melted, and the metal flowed into the space in the desired shape.

THE NEW FIRE CEREMONY

The Aztecs combined a solar calender of 365 days with another 'Sacred Calendar' of 260 days, used for ritual purposes. Every 52 years came a 'Calender Round', a complete cycle of time in both calendars. At this point, the end of an era, the Aztecs believed that the world might end. Five days before the end of the cycle, everyone began to put out their fires, clean their homes, throw away their old clothes and smash all their pots. On the fifth night, people and priests marched to the Hill of the Star, and sacrificed a victim by lighting a fire on his chest and burning his heart. The Aztecs believed that these actions saved the world from destruction.

VULTURE

FIRST KNIFE

FLOWER

HOUSE

RAIN

MOTION

CROCODILE

WIND

DEATH

DEER

RELIGION

THE GREAT TEMPLE

At the centre of Tenochtitlan was the huge temple called the Templo Mayor. It was extended on seven occasions; by the time Moctezuma came to power, it measured more than 90 m by 70 m, and stood 27 m high.

*S*oon after a child was born, its naming ceremony took place. As was usual in Aztec society, guests gave long speeches to the infant. These speeches were often depressing: 'You shall see and know and feel pain, trouble and suffering. This Earth is a place of torment and toil.' The Aztecs believed that both women who died in childbirth and great warriors became gods who helped the sun to go across the heavens. People who died of disease or through accident went to the land of Tlaloc. Everyone else had to suffer torments on the way to Mictlan (the place of the dead), where their souls were destroyed.

SKINNED ALIVE

Aztec gods, like nature, both hurt and helped people. Xipe Totec was the god of fertility, flowers and life. But he also brought skin diseases and eye problems. In one sacrifice to this god, priests killed the victims by shooting arrows at them. Afterwards, they wore the victims' flayed skins, to symbolize the new plants covering the ground in springtime.

THE COYOLXAUHQUI STONE

According to Aztec stories, when Coatlicue was giving birth to the god Huitzilopochtli, her eldest daughter, Coyolxauhqui, climbed the holy mountain to try to kill her mother. Huitzilopochtli leapt from his mother's womb, cut his sister into pieces and threw her down the mountain. This stone, found by archaeologists at the foot of the stairs of the main temple, shows her chopped-up body. The story explains why, after most sacrifices, the victims' bodies were thrown down the temple steps.

PRIESTS OF DEATH

Aztec priests wore black cloaks and grew their nails and hair long. Their hair was matted with blood, and they stank of rotting meat. Their duties were to make sure that all the ceremonies and sacrifices were carried out correctly. Some also taught the young noblemen in a school called the calmecac (see page 20). Others were scribes or astronomers. Aztec priests never married, and were expected to live holy lives.

GIFTS TO NATURE

The Aztecs believed that sacrifices were necessary to make the sun rise again. Huge numbers of victims were killed – 80,400 were said to have been sacrificed at one ceremony alone. Ornate knives, like the one above, were made just for sacrifices.

SACRIFICIAL RITES

This picture shows an Aztec sacrifice. The Aztecs sacrificed people in many different ways. Once, a young man lived as the god Tezcatlipoca for a year; he was given everything he wanted, including four beautiful girls as his wives, but at the end of that year he was sacrificed. On another occasion, captives were thrown into the fire alive but, before they died, were pulled out to have their hearts ripped from them. At the end of another ceremony, people took home the victims' flesh, and ate it in a stew.

AZTEC INFLUENCE

*H*ernan Cortes, the Spaniard
who conquered the Aztecs,
could be accused of destroying
one of the most extraordinary civilizations
in the world. The Aztecs were fierce
warriors and skilled builders, who created a great American
empire. The only bigger one was that of the Incas in Peru.
Aztec society was well organized, and the merchants developed
strong trading links with other peoples. However, in our eyes,
they might seem invaders, who stole the heritage and ideas of
the peoples they conquered. They terrorized the surrounding
cities and sacrificed victims on a grand scale. The Spanish
managed to wipe away most traces of the Aztecs, but their
modern-day descendants, the Nahua,
still live in similar houses and also follow
some of their religious practices.

HISTORICAL HOUSES

Many of the Aztec's descendants still live in houses very similar to the
thatched, mud-brick cottages built by their ancestors. They still use
traditional cooking methods, and practise traditional crafts. More than a
million people speak Nahuatl, the Aztec language.

PYRAMID TRADITION

This is the Pyramid of the Moon at Teotihuacan, source of great
inspiration to the Aztecs. They sought to make their
capital, Tenochtitlan, a worthy successor to
this once great city of towering
pyramids and temples.

4

THE DEATH OF THE AZTECS

On Good Friday in 1519, Hernan Cortes and 600 Spaniards landed on the coast of Mexico. Just three years later, the Aztec Empire had surrendered to them, and the city of Tenochtitlan was in ruins. Aztec weapons and battle tactics could not stop the Spaniards, who were helped by the Aztecs' many enemies. The Aztecs made many sacrifices, but were also laid low by smallpox (which the Aztecs had no immunity to and it spread with extraordinary speed) and were defeated by the Spanish. Their morale collapsed and they lost their confidence because they believed the gods had not supported them.

A NEW RELIGION

The Spaniards quickly destroyed the Aztec religion, and spread the message of Christianity. Many Aztecs were happy to worship a God who did not require constant sacrifice. Today, many Nahua (descendents of the Aztecs) are devout Christians. But traces of the old gods still survive in some modern ceremonies. For instance, the Nahua still spread marigolds on 2 November, though they do so today to celebrate the Christian festival of All Souls' Day, not to honour Xochiquetzal.

GLOSSARY

Aqueduct A structure for carrying water across land, especially one that looks like a high bridge with many arches.

Barbaric To be savagely cruel and extremely brutal.

Captive A person who has been taken as a prisoner. Especially a person held by the enemy during a war.

Glyphs Picture symbols, which were used by the Aztecs to represent the 20 days of the Sacred Calendar.

Gruesome Extremely unpleasant and shocking, and usually dealing with death or injury.

Immune Resistant to a particular infection. The Aztecs were not immune to smallpox.

Nobleman A man that belongs to a noble class.

Mythology A set of stories about the gods and heroes of a particular culture.

Nomad A person that has no permanent home and travels from place to place.

Ritual A set of fixed actions and sometimes words performed regularly, especially as part of a religious ceremony.

Ruin The broken parts that are left from an old building or town.

Sacrifice To kill an animal or a person and offer them to a god or gods.

Tribute A payment in the form of an act or gift. The Aztecs demanded large tributes from cities they conquered.

ACKNOWLEDGEMENTS

We would like to thank: David Drew and Elizabeth Wiggans for their assistance. ·
Artwork by John Alston and David Hobbs
Copyright © 2008 ticktock Entertainment Ltd.
First published in Great Britain by ticktock Media Ltd., Unit 2, Orchard Business Centre, North Farm Road, Tunbridge Wells, Kent, TN2 3XF, UK.
All rights reserved. No part of this publication may be reproduced, stored in a retrieval system, or transmitted in any form or by any means electronic, mechanical, photocopying, recording or otherwise, without prior written permission of the copyright owner.
A CIP catalogue record for this book is available from the British Library.
ISBN 978 1 84696 662 0
Picture research by Image Select. Printed in China.

Picture Credits:
t=top, b=bottom, c=centre, l=left, r=right, OFC=outside front cover, IFC=inside front cover, IBC=inside back cover, OBC=outside back cover

AKG; 2/3c, 2tl & OFC (main pic), 8c, 8/9cb, 11cl, 14tl, 16bl, 17t, 19c, 22bl & OBCtl,. Ancient Art & Architecture; OFCcb, 7br, 12tl, 18/19c, 29cl. Ann Ronan @ Image Select; 13tr. Asia; 10cl. Corbis; 30/31c. Elizabeth Baquedane; 9r, 14b, 18tl, 21br, 22/23c, 24t, 24tl, 28c, 31cr. et archive; OFCr, IFC, 2bl, 3bc, 3br, 5br, 5tr, 6/7c, 7tr, 8bl, 9t, 10br, 11br, 12tl, 13br & OBCcr, 15tl, 16tl, 17cl & OBCb, 19t, 24/25 & 32, 28/29c, p31ct. Image Select; 4c & OFCc, 5br, 20/21 all. Planet Earth Pictures; 27c. Spectrum Colour Library; p8tl. Nick Saunders/Barbara Heller @ Werner Forman; 10cl. Werner Forman; 5c & 29br, 6bm, 10tl, 12ct, 12/13tl, 23cr, 24r, 26tl, 26b, 26/27c, 28bl, 30cl.

Every effort has been made to trace the copyright holders and we apologise in advance for any unintentional omissions.
We would be pleased to insert the appropriate acknowledgement in any subsequent edition of this publication.